EVALUATION OF

COMPLIANCE EXPLAINED

GW00722705

by

David Balkwell

ISO 14001 & OHSAS 18001

COMPLIANT

BALKWELL LTD
ENGLAND
RAISING STANDARDS SINCE 1984

◆

MANAGEMENT SYSTEMS CONSULTANCY, AUDIT & TRAINING

David Balkwell can be contacted at

www.balkwellltd.com

BALKWELL LIMITED
ISOBUILDER®

Published by

Balkwell Limited - ISOBUILDER®

Cavendish House

Welbeck

Nottinghamshire

S80 3LL

UK

Email: office@balkwellltd.com

www.balkwellltd.com

First Published 2013

Copyright © David Balkwell 2013

ISBN   978-0-9576245-0-4

Printed in England.

pleased in such cases to place an acknowledgment in future editions of the publication.

Interpretations of International and local Standards are limited and therefore other similar methodologies may exist to those contained in this publication.

ISOBUILDER® is a Registered Trade Mark of Balkwell Ltd

"TEOC Approach™" is protected by copyright and our ISOBUILDER® Registered Trade Mark.

All images created by S. Irons

CONTENTS

BALKWELL LTD
ENGLAND
RAISING STANDARDS SINCE 1984

◆

MANAGEMENT SYSTEMS CONSULTANCY, AUDIT & TRAINING

For further information on this and other

ISOBUILDER® Books & Tools

visit www.balkwellltd.com

●

ACKNOWLEDGEMENTS

This book would never have happened without the special help of my immediate family, Crystal, Zoë, my Mother and Mother and Father in Law - thank you for your tolerance and patience.

My thanks to friends and colleagues with whom I have had the pleasure of working with in the field of Management Systems over the years.

Scott for the long awaited images and finally Zoë for her editorial.

●

THE AUTHOR

David Balkwell
BSc, FFB, MCMI, ABEng

Member of the Society of Construction Law

Quality - Environmental - Health & Safety Registered

Lead Assessor

Founder of Balkwell Limited & *ISOBUILDER*®

David Balkwell is a much sought after expert on the subject of Management Systems – ISO 9001 ISO 14001 OHSAS 18001. He is one of only a very few active certification body assessors on the public speaking circuit; and he supports hundreds of leaders involved in Management Systems each year.

David studied and gained a Bachelor of Science Degree in Building at Coventry (Lanchester) Polytechnic. He is a lifetime member of Coventry University Alumni.

He began his working life with a short spell in the drinks industry however quickly moved on to be a Junior Archaeologist in the Roman

City of Chester. He soon became Chester City Museum Assistant Photographer.

For five years, he was a Building Regulator at Sheffield Metropolitan District Council (1984 to 1989) responsible for Property Compliance Inspections, Dangerous Structures, Safety at Sports Grounds and Public Premises Licensing.

For over ten years, he was a Certification Lead Assessor Operations Manager for The British Standards Institution (BSI) where he managed a team of 20 multidisciplinary lead assessors.

It was there he developed his management systems skills based upon a detailed grounding in compliance.

One of his last achievements in BSI was to be the co-founder of OHSAS 18001:1999.

David carried out the first BSI "Integrated Assessment" QMS & EMS David carried out in 1995, since then he has undertaken hundreds of combined audits and Management Systems Certification Assessments.

Since 1999 he has run his own business – Specialising in Management System Consultancy, Audit and Training.

David has been a significant contributor to: PAS 99 (Specification of common management system requirements as a framework for integration), ISO 22000 and PAS 7 (Forthcoming Fire risk management system - Specification).

During his time at BSI and since, he has been responsible for the development and/or assessment of organisations goals to build better business through management systems.

He has delivered his expertise around the world, including:

Japan, Saudi Arabia, Syria, United Kingdom, Ireland, Malaysia, Indonesia, Russia, Sri Lanka, Sweden, Belgium, Gibraltar, Turkey, Italy, France, USA, Mexico, Egypt, Ascension Island, Australia, New Zealand, Kazakhstan, Ukraine, Falkland Islands, Norway, Spain, Finland Etc.

David has over 4000 days of Certification Assessment experience to share, accrued over the last 23 years.

David's Qualifications Include:

- BSc. in Building Construction

- Fellow of the Faculty of Building – FFB

- Full Member of the Institute of Management – MCMI

- Member of the Society of Construction Law

- IRCA ISO 9001 QMS Lead Assessor

- IEMA ISO 14001 EMS Lead Assessor

- ASCB(E) OHSAS 18001 HSS Lead Assessor

- SA 8000 Auditor

- ISO 55001 Lead Assessor

- NHSS 2a,b,c, 12a/b,c,d, 8, 18 Specialist Lead Assessor

●
ABOUT
Balkwell Limited – *ISOBUILDER*®

Balkwell Limited's professional consultants offer an integrated service of auditing and management system implementations, assessments, training and *ISOBUILDER*® Management Systems Support Tools.

We provide local and overseas Companies with an all-round service. The hallmark of Balkwell Limited's success is the volume of repeat business we do with our clients.

We deliver Training across a range of subjects including Quality, Environment, Health & Safety, Integration, Social Accountability and National Highways Sector Schemes etc, which can be provided, either in-house or tailored to your needs.

Balkwell Limited are specialists in Management Systems. We know exactly what the standards require and what the Certification Bodies are looking for.

With over 23 years of Management Systems experience, we are a world leader.

We have designed and implemented many Integrated Management Systems (IMS's) of up to five different Management Systems into one Integrated Management System.

David has performed certification assessments on behalf of 10 different certification bodies across a range of disciplines, such as ISO 9001 including several National Highway Sector Schemes, ISO 14001, OHSAS 18001, PAS 55 and PAS 99.

●

FIGURES

For the benefit of purchasers of this book we have made available a set of useable templates:

- Sample Legal and Other Compliance Procedure
- Sample Evaluation of Compliance Procedure
- Sample Legislation Register
- Evaluation of Compliance Plan
- Evidence by Location
- Sample Evaluation of Compliance Report
- Sample Evaluation of Compliance Findings Report

Please note the samples do not contain Company related information, such as legislation. We have no knowledge of what your Organisation does, however are more than happy to supply the sample templates to give you a start.

For your sample templates contact David Balkwell at

www.balkwellltd.com

CHAPTER 1
INTRODUCTION

Evaluation of Compliance has been unexplained and misunderstood for over 9 years.

So, I have written this book to share with you what needs be done to meet the requirements of ISO 14001 & OHSAS 18001's - Evaluation of Compliance.

Throughout this book I may make reference to legal requirements – where legal and other requirements are in fact intended.

If you are safety or environmental management systems aware, you may well have developed a Legal Register. This could be in various formats with links to each piece of legislation giving you a direct connection to legal and other requirements applicable to your Organisation.

However you will need to go further to meet compliance to ISO 14001 and or OHSAS 18001, the register on its own won't satisfy the Auditor's or your Legal Obligation.

Certification Bodies are only required to audit conformity with the Standard; they are not required to make a direct evaluation of Legal Compliance since this is an Organisation's Legal Duty.

I will explain further...

It is the Organisations responsibility to ensure that a periodic evaluation of compliance, with each applicable legal and other requirement is undertaken. From this, the Auditor should be able to determine whether the organisation has established the necessary procedures and has evaluated the requirements in enough depth to demonstrate legal and other requirements compliance and compliance with the intent of Evaluation of Compliance in ISO 14001 and OHSAS 18001.

I would go onto say in some instances compliance may involve maintenance of records i.e. Statutory Inspections. You will need to show *'who has that duty and/or where those records are kept'*. This could possibly be on the legal register or certainly somewhere in the management system.

The evaluation process is very similar to an internal audit, however, you will need to pay particular attention to the legislative requirements and other requirements for a given process or activity to be able to show they are being effectively met.

The Auditor will expect to see these and will want to check the Organisations evaluations.

You should therefore include documents to show how your evaluations were made, with sampled records, references and examples of compliance to specific legal duties.

So, simple documents such as waste transfer notes, Statutory Inspections, etc. referenced back to working procedures and practices, is a good starting point.

In summary the Organisation will need to show an evaluation process and over a specified period of time this process must cover all of the applicable legal and other requirements.

Here at Balkwell Consulting - ISOBUILDER® we have developed a suitable and compliant process, which enables you to check and confirm that staff understand the legal and other requirements and to demonstrate good practice.

David Balkwell

●

CHAPTER 2
WHAT IS A MANAGEMENT SYSTEM

In relation to Evaluation of Compliance, this Chapter is designed to outline the higher level management system structure.

A systematic, logical approach to business management is essential if you are to operate a lean, effective and successful business. Many tools are available to achieve this; however selection of the right tool is not "Magic Dust" or a "Wonder Drug".

Quality, Environment and Health & Safety are fundamental philosophies in any organisation.

Quality is of course crucial; not only to stay in business but to ensure customers get what they ask for.

Environment, although more a modern philosophy, is about an Organisations impact on the rest of the world. Where we position ourselves as an Organisation, not only helps us comply with requirements, legislation, and anything else we choose to subscribe to, but also sends messages beyond the Organisation, communicating our Environmental position.

Health & Safety is about the Organisation and its employees, visitors and stakeholders who are in direct contact with the building or site. Also there are issues with compliance and legal responsibilities, as with Environment.

There are management systems for many disciplines i.e. Quality, Environment, Health & Safety, Information Security, Complaints Handling, Aerospace, Telecommunication, Food Safety, Automotive, etc. The principles all of which are based on Plan Do Check Act (PDCA).

What is a Management System

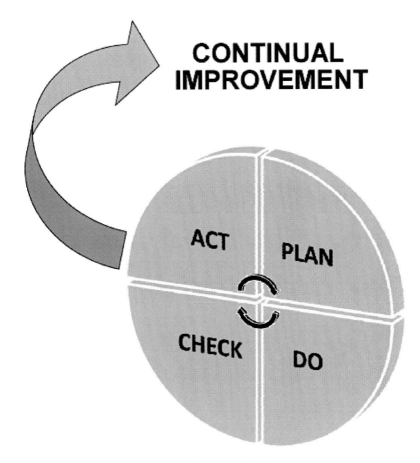

Figure 1 Plan Do Check Act Cycle (PDCA)

The principle of Plan Do Check Act is well known and long established within management systems.

What is a Management System

The PDCA model was made popular by Dr. W. Edwards Deming, who is considered by many to be the father of modern quality control. Later in Deming's career, he modified PDCA to "Plan, Do, Study, Act" (PDSA) because he felt that "check" emphasized inspection over analysis, however he referred to the model as the "Shewhart Cycle"

Typically in the world of management systems, the term "Check" is preferred.

PDCA Explained…

Plan – Establish baselines, analyze your organization's situation, create your overall policy, objectives, set your targets, develop plans to achieve them, whilst evaluating and prioritizing risk at all times. For Health and Safety and Environmental management systems, identify applicable legislation and other requirements – Not forgetting management programme/s for Environmental.

Do – Implement your plans (do what you planned to do).

Check – Measure your results (measure/monitor how far your actual achievements meet your planned objectives and targets, including **Evaluation of Compliance**).

Act – Through Management Review, the intent is to demonstrate suitability, adequacy and effectiveness of the management system and

8

ultimately show Continual Improvement. Correct and improve your plans and how you put them into practice (correct and learn from your mistakes to improve your plans in order to achieve better results next time).

A management system is the framework of processes and procedures used to ensure that an organization can fulfil all tasks required to achieve its objectives.

What can you expect in return for your investment in a Management System?

Feedback from management systems certified companies shows you can expect payoff from all of your hard work.

Because of the responsibilities requirements in ISO 9001 (Clause 5), organizations often see an increased involvement of top management with regards to the quality management system and the same subsequently with multiple systems.

This starts with the setting of the Policy and Objectives based on determination of risk with respect to Quality, Environment and Health & Safety. It continues with Management Review, looking at data output from the Integrated Management System (IMS), and taking actions to make sure that objectives and targets are met, new objectives and targets are set, and continual improvement is achieved.

With the IMS in place and working for you, the organization is focused towards the objectives and targets and continual improvement. Management is provided with data on a continual basis and are able to see progress or lack of progress towards objectives and targets, and take appropriate action. The process of conducting management review ensures that this evaluation takes place. It provides the mechanism of reviewing outputs from the management system as inputs on a scheduled basis, and for taking action based on the evaluation.

Increased productivity is a result of the initial evaluation and ongoing improvement of processes, and from improved training and competence of employees.

Better documentation or control of processes leads to consistency in performance, less waste and rework. Managers experience fewer late night TROUBLESHOOTING calls; employees have more information for solving problems on their own.

As customer satisfaction improves, the more customers needs are taken into account. Customer needs are better understood as customer feedback is sought, received and analyzed. Objectives and targets are

What is a Management System

adjusted based on the information produced and the organisation becomes more customer driven. As objectives focus on the customer and risk, the organization spends less time focusing on individual objectives of departments and more time working together to meet customer needs and reducing environmental and health and safety impacts.

All of this leads to financial rewards, reward for your hard work and investment in the Integrated Management System. So work with enthusiasm and optimism, knowing that your organization will be significantly improved by IMS implementation. You are contributing to the future success and profitability of your Organisation.

When ISO 9001 / ISO 14001 / OHSAS 18001 are implemented in an Organization, you can expect the following:

- Well defined and documented procedures and processes improving the consistency of output
- Quality, Environmental and Health & Safety performance is constantly measured
- Procedures/Processes ensure corrective and preventive action is taken whenever defects or non-compliance occurs
- Defect rates decrease
- Improved compliance and supporting objective evidence

What is a Management System

- Defects are caught earlier and are corrected at a lower cost
- Better legal and other requirements identification, management and compliance
- Defining procedures identifies current practices that are obsolete or inefficient
- Reduced waste
- Improved Safety
- Documented procedures are easier for new employees to follow
- Improved incident management and preparedness
- Organizations retain or increase market share, increasing sales or revenues

Top reasons given for Registration / Certification:

- Improved legal and other requirements compliance
- Internal operational efficiency
- Lower production costs because of fewer nonconforming products, less rework, lowered rejection rates, streamlined processes and fewer mistakes.
- Access to new markets
- Some markets demand or favour ISO 9001 / ISO 14001 / OHSAS 18001 Certification

What is a Management System

- Many organizations are asked by a customer to obtain registration as a requirement to continue or to start doing business with them.
- Better process control and flow
- Improved documentation quality
- Greater employee quality/environmental/health & safety awareness
- Reductions in product scrap, reworks and rejections

There is an important point to consider at this stage and that is the principle of the process approach in ISO 9001, and how that can be used to demonstrate the relationship between legal management and evaluation of compliance.

The principle builds on PDCA and INPUT, PROCESS, OUTPUT…

To improve one's understanding of management systems, this is a simple test. Challenge an individual clause…

INPUT ➔ Where does it come from?
PROCESS ➔ What does it do?
OUTPUT ➔ Where does it go to?

So how does this work - consider Legal management…

INPUT ➜ Where does it come from?
- It's the Law of the Land
- There is a clause in the Standards which expect it
- The Standards Policy Statements expect it

PROCESS ➜ What does it do?
- It defines the approach to the management of Legislation and other requirements – i.e. the process or procedure

OUTPUT ➜ Where does it go to?
- Risk Assessment and Aspect Evaluation in determination of the significance of Risk

Now you can apply the same test to Evaluation of Compliance!

Have a think about it… (The answer is at the back of this book)

The more you do this, the more you will understand about Management Systems – in fact for every clause of any of the management systems standards, this can be applied.

You will find there is a higher level relationship between legal management and Evaluation of Compliance.

14
What is a Management System

CHAPTER 3

UNDERSTANDING LEGAL & OTHER REQUIREMENTS MANAGEMENT

Health, Safety and Environmental legislation in the UK is enforced by the Health & Safety Executive and the Environment Agency in England and Wales, the Scottish Environment Protection Agency in Scotland and the Northern Ireland Environment and Heritage Service in Northern Ireland.

There are other regulatory bodies of course, including Local Authorities.

An Employers' Duties include:

- Ensuring that management responsibilities in relation to compliance are clearly defined
- Ensuring that the relevant management representative has a properly executed job description and is allocated the resources necessary to ensure compliance
- Identify and Maintain access to (usually a register) relevant legislation and other requirements

15
Understanding Legal & Other Requirements Management

- Ensuring that access is provided to legal briefing or other services which will ensure that the register is maintained and updated with changes or additional legislation
- Ensuring that relevant parts of the organisation are briefed on the requirements of the relevant legislation and other requirements
- Providing access for regulatory inspections, as necessary

Employees' Duties include:

- Being aware of legislation affecting operations
- Operating and maintaining processes to keep controlled impacts within regulatory limits
- Notifying management where operations threaten to compromise legal compliance
- Notifying management when compliance limits have been exceeded
- Ensuring that contractors and service providers work within the organisation's management system to maintain compliance

In Practice;

ISO 14001 requires an organisation to:

"establish, implement and maintain procedures to: (a) identify and have access to the applicable legal requirements and other requirements to which the organisation subscribes related to its environmental aspects, and (b) determine how these requirements apply to its environmental aspects."

The standard goes on to specify the need for applicable legislation and other requirements to be incorporated into the environmental management system.

OHSAS18001 requires an organisation to:

"establish, implement and maintain a procedure(s) for identifying and accessing the legal and other OH&S requirements that are applicable to it.

The organization shall ensure that these applicable legal requirements and other requirements to which the organization subscribes are taken into account in establishing, implementing and maintaining its OH&S management system."

The organization shall keep this information up-to-date.

The organization shall communicate relevant information on legal and other requirements to persons working under the control of the Organisation, and other relevant interested parties.

Here are some examples of what needs to be included.....

Legal requirements can take many forms, such as:

Legislation, including statutes, regulations and codes of practice:
- Decrees and directives
- Orders issued by regulators
- Permits, licences or other forms of authorization
- Judgements of courts or administrative tribunals
- Treaties, conventions, protocols

Examples of "Other requirements" can include:
- Contractual conditions
- Agreements with employees
- Agreements with interested parties
- Agreements with health authorities
- Non-regulatory guidelines
- Voluntary principles, best practices or codes of practice, charters

Understanding Legal & Other Requirements Management

- Local Authority initiatives

- Trade Association Charters

- Public commitments of the organization or its parent organization, and Corporate / Organisation *requirements*.

Understanding Legal & Other Requirements Management

Legislation Register

AREA	LEGISLATION	REVIEW DATE	BRIEF DESCRIPTION	HOW / WHERE DOES IT APPLY
Environment Nuisance	Noise and Statutory Nuisance Act 1993	April 2013	Establishes the regime for controlling noise	The company's activities do not cause a statutory nuisance. The company is located in an industrial area, but there is a public park opposite. The nearest residential properties are ¼ mile away.
Waste	The Waste (England & Wales) Regulations SI2011/988 and amendment SI2012/1889	April 2013	The regulation sets out a framework for evaluating, controlling and removal of waste	All waste to be evaluated before the waste is taken from site to comply with Regulation 12 very effort to reduce, recycle, reuse etc
Manual Handling	Manual Handling Operations Regulations SI1999/2793	April 2013	Manual handling operations means any transporting or supporting of a load (including lifting, putting down, pushing, pulling, carrying or moving it) by hand or by bodily force. There is a general duty on employers to avoid the need for manual handling	In the workshops and out on site
PPE	Construction (Head Protection) Regulations SI1989/2009	April 2013	The aim of the Regulations is to make sure that people working on construction sites wears suitable head protection.	Wherever there is a risk of head injuries

Figure 2 Sample Legislation Register

An important step in achieving best practice is to establish against the register of applicable legislation and other requirements a level of significance of each entry to the Organisation, hence the "SIG" column in Figure 4.

Of course there are a number of ways to do this, employ a suitably knowledgeable individual to carry out the exercise, subcontract the task, or do it yourselves. This does not absolve the fact that the Organisation should have adequate knowledge of each of the entries in the register to ensure compliance – so you could in principle do it yourselves. Either way, keep it simple!

It may be sufficient to gather a group of people together in the organisation who have knowledge of each of the entries on the register and give each attendee three pieces of paper each with HIGH, MEDIUM and LOW on, and systematically ask against each entry for them to rank based on their individual knowledge.

Don't forget however to ensure this is an integral part of the procedure for legal and other requirements management.

Also to make this process effective the ranking needs to be reviewed as you would update to the register.

Understanding Legal & Other Requirements Management

Although we have shown a very simple example (Figure 2), the legislation register could also:

- List all legislation applicable to the organisation and its activities
- List all other requirements applicable to the organisation and its activities
- Where possible, state the impact of each item of legislation on the organisation, any criminal liability for breaches of the legislation, and the relevant regulator concerned
- Be updated on a regular basis — any changes should be communicated to the relevant people within the organisation
- Be maintained and managed centrally, either as a standalone document or as part of the impact/risk register, to ensure accuracy and avoid duplication

Keeping the Register up to date:

The sources of information used to keep the register up to date will vary according to the organisation's activities and resources. They may include the following:

- Official government websites, e.g. Environment Agency, HSE, Defra, DTI

Understanding Legal & Other Requirements Management

- Staff and/or corporate membership of professional bodies, e.g. IEMA, Chartered Institution of Water and Environmental Management, Society for the Environment, Chartered Institution of Wastes Management, IOSH, Institute of Ecology and Environmental Management, UK Environmental Law Association, Engineering Employers' Federation, Chemical Industries Association
- Specialist online services also exist, e.g. iSOS™ Plus and ISOBUILDER® Legislation Manager, The British Library Directories, handbooks and loose-leaf publications
- Related magazines and journals

There should be a procedure for maintaining the legislation and other requirements register which sets out roles and responsibilities, review periods, etc.

Contact us for your free sample procedure.

It is noted that the related standards do not suggest, unlike many references in ISO 9001, that the procedure is documented.

However, ISO 14001 and OHSAS 18001 do not mention "documented", so how do you ensure effective replication of ongoing control of the process? I will leave that thought with you…

Changes to the register should be communicated to the relevant people in the organisation.

TOP TIP......

" GOOD EVALUATION OF COMPLIANCE IS ONLY AS GOOD AS THE PROCESS OF LEGAL AND OTHER REQUIREMENTS MANAGEMENT.

I.E. THE BETTER THE APPLICABLE LEGISLATION AND OTHER REQUIREMENTS ARE UNDERSTOOD AND EMBRACED AT THE PLAN STAGE THE EASIER THE EVALUATION OF COMPLIANCE IS IN THE CHECK STAGE. "

CHAPTER 4
WHY WAS EVALUATION OF
COMPLIANCE INTRODUCED

All standards, management systems having no exception, are reviewed on a regular basis. As a broad rule they are reviewed every 7 years or so.

During the review of the 1996 ISO 14001 standard a number of questions were asked of the users, one being; "Do you believe that compliance with ISO 14001 improves your legal compliance?"

A significant number responded that they did not believe it did improve compliance!

Interestingly, within the existing clause in the standard monitoring and measurement, there was a requirement to monitor and measure legal compliance. However it would appear that this was not robustly implemented or challenged during the life of the Standard.

So in response to this concern it was decided to remove the requirement from monitoring and measurement and give it a clause of its own.

Many questions have since been asked about the purpose and the intent of evaluation of compliance – this book endeavours to provide an explanation and some solutions.

TOP TIP......

" DON'T THINK OF EVALUATION OF COMPLIANCE AS A PART OF INTERNAL AUDIT OR MONITORING AND MEASUREMENT AND ENDEAVOUR TO RESPOND TO THE REQUIREMENT IN ISOLATION AS A CLAUSE IN ITS OWN RIGHT WHICH IS EXACTLY WHAT IT IS IN THE STANDARDS. "

Why Was Evaluation of Compliance Introduced

CHAPTER 5
WHAT IS EVALUATION OF COMPLIANCE

ISO 14001 and OHSAS 18001 both contain a clause called Evaluation of Compliance. This clause has been separated from '*4.5.1 – Monitoring and Measurement'* and includes two sub-clauses, as well as clarification as an addition to the ISO 14001:1996 standard.

Included in Clause 4.5.1 of ISO 14001:1996 was a requirement for the organisation to periodically evaluate compliance with relevant (now applicable) environmental legislation and regulations.

This requirement has been retained in Clause 4.5.2.1 of the revised standard. In Clause 4.5.2.2, ISO 14001 includes evaluation of compliance with legal and other requirements to which the organisation subscribes, which was not specifically required by ISO 14001:1996.

This clarification also includes a requirement for records of periodic evaluations of compliance to be kept.

There is an opinion that compliance against each and every piece of legislation or regulation relating to an organisation which would need to be evaluated before it can be considered to be in conformity with ISO 14001. It will not be acceptable for organisations to claim that the periodic evaluation will be covered by their traditional internal audit process.

This has always been one of the most difficult issues in ISO 14001, and subsequently OHSAS 18001 and organisations will need to review and revise their compliance procedures to ensure that they meet and continue to meet, these requirements.

Clause 4.5.2 within ISO 14001:2004 and OHSAS 18001:2007 is often found to be a weakness within an Organisation's system's and in most cases the process is not fully understood. This book endeavours to unravel this.

While certification of a Health & Safety and Environmental Management System against the requirements of ISO 14001:2004 or OHSAS 18001:2007 is not a guarantee of legal compliance, it is a proven and efficient tool in achieving and maintaining such legal and other requirements compliance.

What is Evaluation of Compliance

ISO 14001:2004 or OHSAS 18001:2007 certification should demonstrate that an independent third-party (Certification Body) has evaluated and confirmed that the organisation has a demonstrably effective EMS or H&SS to ensure the fulfilment of its policy commitments including legal and other requirements compliance.

Certification Body auditors are required to audit conformity of an EMS or H&SS to the requirements of ISO 14001:2004 or OHSAS 18001:2007. They are not required to make a direct evaluation of legal compliance since this is the requirement for the organisation nor is the auditor required to conduct a compliance audit, which would be the role of the regulator or an auditor/inspector contracted specifically for this purpose.

It is the organisation's responsibility, and a function of the EMS or H&SS, to ensure that the organisation periodically evaluates compliance with each and every applicable legal and other requirement, and it is aware of its compliance status. An EMS or H&SS certified as meeting the requirements of ISO 14001:2004 or OHSAS 18001:2007 is expected to be able to identify the organisation's compliance status. Although not a requirement directly of the standards, it is the only way to demonstrate at any given time, the current level of effectiveness of the Evaluation of Compliance process.

What is Evaluation of Compliance

The auditor should be able to determine whether the organisation has established that the necessary procedures exist and has evaluated the legal compliance and other requirements in sufficient depth to demonstrate compliance.

Contact us for your free sample procedure.

An Integrated Management System (IMS) Auditor will evaluate the effectiveness of the organisations evaluation through:

- Sampling the organisation's determination of compliance with examples of specific legal and other requirements compliance
- Looking for evidence of compliance, such as reviewing waste transfer documentation, lifting certificates
- Reviewing the organisations evaluation process to ensure that the process has or will have covered all legal and other requirements
- Verifying the capability of the evaluation, this may be through the competencies of the personnel performing the evaluations

The responsibility for compliance stays with the organisation; therefore the evaluation process you perform is significant to the effectiveness of your EMS or H&SS Systems.

What is Evaluation of Compliance

The evaluation process is similar to an internal audit process but the organisation should pay specific attention to the legislative and other requirements and if they are being effectively met.

It can become extremely difficult however to manage the process of evaluation of compliance when it is a part of internal audit.

As an example; waste transfer notes are currently required to be retained (in the UK) for 2 years for non hazardous waste and 3 years for hazardous, you also need to ensure that the organisation taking the waste is licensed and takes the waste to a licensed facility for that type of waste etc. To evaluate compliance to this, an auditor could select a number of waste transfer notes for the different types of waste streams within the organisation, ensuring that the records are available, the person taking/collecting the waste has a valid waste carrier license and there is a copy of the waste management license/environmental permit for the disposal site which is valid for the type of waste received.

The difficulty is, the example could be covered through internal audit, monitoring and measurement or structured evaluation of compliance.

The simple rule is; the decision to use internal audit, monitoring and measurement or structured evaluation of compliance should be based on

What is Evaluation of Compliance

the size, scale and complexity of the organisation and the subsequent significance of Health and Safety, and Environmental impact.

The evaluation notes/evidence should be able to clearly demonstrate that documents and records have been reviewed and are satisfactory for ensuring legal and other requirements compliance.

There is not necessarily a right or wrong way of evaluating your legal compliance but the auditor should have confidence in the system that has been implemented.

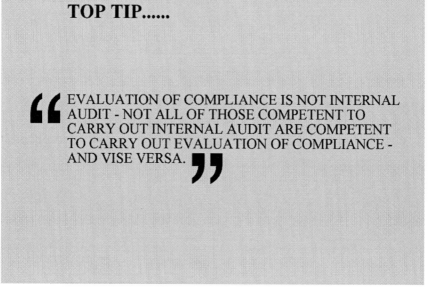

TOP TIP......

" EVALUATION OF COMPLIANCE IS NOT INTERNAL AUDIT - NOT ALL OF THOSE COMPETENT TO CARRY OUT INTERNAL AUDIT ARE COMPETENT TO CARRY OUT EVALUATION OF COMPLIANCE - AND VISE VERSA. "

What is Evaluation of Compliance

CHAPTER 6
DIFFERENT TYPES OF EVALUATION
OF COMPLIANCE

So, Evaluation of Compliance can be demonstrated in a number of ways:

- Evaluation of Compliance as a function on its own
- Thorough Monitoring and Measurement
- Thorough Internal Audit
- Λ combination of above

The chosen approach is of course the responsibility of the Organisation needing to achieve and demonstrate evaluation of compliance. However, as previously discussed to provide the most clarity undertake evaluation of compliance as a function on its own. That's how it was intended in the standard. It should be appreciated in many cases to avoid duplication; a blend of the three is likely.

EVALUATION OF COMPLIANCE AS A FUNCTION ON ITS OWN
It is crucial that we create a procedure based approach in line with the intent of the standards and provide suitably competent resource.

Although it is accepted that there may be elements of internal audit output and monitoring and measurement output, which could contribute to compliance with evaluation of compliance, it requires careful planning and suitable resourcing to be effective.

When carried out as a process in its own right we need to challenge systematically each and every identified piece of legislation and other requirement, and provide suitable objective evidence of compliance.

USING MONITORING AND MEASUREMENT
Well it was here where the problem began. It is important that monitoring and measurement activities are not clouded by the principles of evaluation of compliance.

Monitoring and measurement in the standards has an important role in its own right and may include monitoring and measurement of legal and other requirements impact, on the other hand it may not i.e. general site walk abouts or housekeeping checks.

Monitoring and measurement are often used interchangeably, but they do have different meanings.
Monitoring: is the regular surveillance of the state of a process or a condition.

Different Types of Evaluation of Compliance

Measurement: is the acquisition of quantitative data on the physical, chemical or biological components of a process or condition.

Monitoring does not usually produce accurate, precise, quantified data on a process, but typically does not need to do so, as an inference about a process may be sufficient and indicate a need for measurements.

EMPLOYERS' DUTIES
- It is important to inform staff of auditing and monitoring/ measurement schedules
- Provide competent auditors
- Make records available to those who need to see them, such as third party auditors and regulators

EMPLOYEES' DUTIES
- Co-operate during audits and monitoring/measurement programmes
- Provide records in a timely manner to those who need to see them

Different Types of Evaluation of Compliance

The table below shows some examples of processes and how they may be monitored or measured

Process	Monitoring	Measuring
Particulate emissions from a boiler	The colour of the emissions and whether particulate matter is emitted in significant amounts	The concentration of particulates in mg/m3
Emissions of odorous substances from an effluent treatment works	Whether a site operative can smell any odorous substances at the site boundary	Measuring the concentrations of specific odorous compounds in the ambient air
Processing cardboard for recycling	Counting the number of filled skips of cardboard sent for recycling	Weighing the cardboard sent for recycling, in kg per month
Discharges of effluent into a river from a process	Grading the flow of effluent visually, using characteristics such as low to high flow rates, and colour of discharges	Measuring the concentrations of specific substances each day, in mg/l, and measuring the flow rates and volumetric flow per day, to quantify the discharges
Production of waste	Counting the number of skips sent to landfill in a year	Weighing the types of waste sent to landfill, in kg/week
Emissions of solvents from a coatings process	Counting the number of drums of solvent used during a given period	Concentrations of solvents in mg/m3. When combined with measurements of volumetric flow, mass emission rates over a given period

Figure 3 Examples of Monitoring & Measurement

Different Types of Evaluation of Compliance

An organisation needs a set of linked and systematic processes and procedures for:

The Monitoring and measurement of significant environmental aspects and impacts, health and safety risks and be able to demonstrate monitoring progress against objectives and targets including monitoring compliance with legally binding limits.

Also there is a need to check whether it is complying with the requirements of ISO 14001 and or OHSAS 18001, applied through its processes, procedures and documented objectives and targets. These checks are performed typically through auditing.

If audits reveal non-compliances — also known as non-conformances or non-conformities — then the organisation must fix the failure, determine why the non-compliance has happened, and then take steps to prevent the recurrence.

Requirements of ISO 14001 for Checking and Review:
The list below summarises the requirements of the checking and review sections of ISO 14001

Different Types of Evaluation of Compliance

CHECKING REQUIREMENTS OF ISO 14001

Clause	Scope	Requirements
4.5.1	Monitoring and measurement	Have procedures for monitoring and measuring key performance characteristics, releases to air, land and water, significant environmental aspects, health and safety risk and progress against objectives and targets. Ensure that any measurements meet the appropriate standards for quality / environment / health and safety. Keep records of monitoring and measurements.
4.5.2	Evaluation of Compliance	Have procedures for periodically assessing compliance with legal and other requirements, especially for legally binding limits for releases to air, land, water etc.
4.5.3	Corrective and Preventive Action	Have procedures for: Identifying non-compliances Correcting non-compliances Determining the causes of the non-compliances Applying or changing procedures to ensure that they do not happen again

Different Types of Evaluation of Compliance

4.5.4	Records	Have procedures for controlling records, including maintenance, retrieval, storage, archiving and disposal.
		Keep and maintain records to provide evidence to show compliance with the EMS and H&SS.
4.5.5	Internal Audits	Have procedures for:
		Internal audits, with audit scopes and schedules based on the relative importance of the process to be audited.
		Selecting auditors with at least sufficient training and experience.
		Reporting the results of audits to management.
4.6	Management Review	Carry out Management reviews at specified intervals to assess the suitability adequacy and effectiveness of the management system, to include a review of progress against objectives and targets, policy, new requirements such as revised laws, audits, and any changes needed – Continual improvement needs to be demonstrated.
		And most importantly review evidence of effective Evaluation of Compliance.

Different Types of Evaluation of Compliance

The same applies for OHSAS 18001 with limited exceptions relating to 4.5.3 where accident management and near miss reporting is covered.

OHSAS 18001:2007 & ISO 14001:2004 are now process-based following alignment with ISO 9001:2008, so an EMS and H&SS have to show the linkages between different processes. This can be easily demonstrated by adopting the "process approach" using the process map technique, process mapping can highlight critical points or stages in the process and consequently where impacts (Critical Control Points) are and where monitoring is required. There should be a logical sequence from impacts identification and evaluation through to operational control to meet objectives and targets.

MONITORING METHODS AND THE QUALITY ASSURANCE OF MONITORING:

Clause 4.5.1 of ISO 14001 also requires monitoring equipment to be managed and calibrated appropriately. Many monitoring standards include provisions for quality assurance, as well as addressing measurement uncertainty. This is a combination of the accuracy and precision of a measurement.

There are benefits in reducing the uncertainty of a measurement, e.g. minimising the chances of false breaches of legal limits, better process

Different Types of Evaluation of Compliance

optimisation, meaning greater efficiency and greater control over environmental aspects and health and safety impacts.

For a piece of measuring equipment, the uncertainty is affected by characteristics such as it's:

- Linearity
- Bias
- Responsiveness to changes in the value
- Resolution
- Repeatability
- Cross-sensitivity to other determinants drift over time
- Effects of environmental or safety conditions.

If these factors can be characterised and understood, then the quality of measurements can be improved. To this end, the International Organization for Standardization (ISO) has published ISO 10012 to support the monitoring and measurement sections of management systems standards such as ISO 14001 and OHSAS 18001.

If an organisation uses all, or even parts of ISO 10012, then its management system will be improved because the monitoring provisions will be strengthened.

Different Types of Evaluation of Compliance

For each piece of measuring equipment, it is recommended that the following information is recorded in line with the related procedures or work instructions:

- Characterisation of performance characteristics (refer to ISO 10012 and the manufacturers specifications)
- Determination of the measurement uncertainty
- Maintenance frequencies
- Calibration methods and schedules
- Evidence of traceability
- Evaluation of Compliance

As we now know, OHSAS 18001 and ISO 14001 requires organisations to have a procedure for assessing compliance with respect to applicable legislation and requirements.

Evaluation of Compliance can best be described as a form of auditing; however it must not be confused with the process of evaluation of compliance.

USING INTERNAL AUDIT - GENERAL GUIDANCE

Internal Audit can be used to fulfil the evaluation of compliance requirement however not all internal auditors have the right skill set or

Different Types of Evaluation of Compliance

the legal knowledge to carry out evaluation of compliance – If this is the chosen approach then care needs to be taken to ensure those selected have the right skill set or if not are provided with suitable training.

AUDITING

Classes and Types of Audits for ISO 14001& OHSAS 18001

Audits can be divided into three classes and within these classes; there are also different types of audit. In simple terms, audit classes are as follows.

FIRST PARTY AUDITS: audits performed by the organisation on itself, also known as internal audits. These are explicitly required by ISO 9001, ISO 14001 and OHSAS 18001

SECOND PARTY AUDITS: an organisation typically performs these on its suppliers. ISO 9001, ISO 14001 and OHSAS 18001 requires these implicitly, as the standard requires the organisation to exert an influence or control over its direct and indirect impacts.

THIRD PARTY AUDITS: these are performed by a Certification Body when assessing the organisation for certification to a standard/s.

Different Types of Evaluation of Compliance

Audits may also be horizontal or vertical, and each of these may be compliance or systems audits.

HORIZONTAL AUDITS: these take a sample of procedures in the management system — such as those for operational control — and then determine compliance with the procedures for a sample of sections within the organisation.

VERTICAL AUDITS: a vertical audit examines a set of linked activities, their component processes and then audits through these vertically in a planned manner.

EVALUATION OF COMPLIANCE AUDITS: examine whether an organisation is meeting a specified legal or other requirement condition, or not.

SYSTEMS AUDITS: develop trails of connected processes, whether planned to follow a specific progression, or according to the findings of the audit as it progresses.

Regulatory officers typically perform compliance audits, but such an approach is not always beneficial to the organisation if it wants to

Different Types of Evaluation of Compliance

improve the management system and its performance. However, a regulator's job is simply to assess compliance.

This simple guidance works for both Internal Audit and Evaluation of Compliance.

IMPORTANT POINT - Choose your audit team.

You will want to have a number of trained auditors for fulfillment of your audit/compliance program. You will be auditing each area of your facility once or twice a year, with an audit team of 1 to 4 auditors depending on the size of the area and its complexity. You will want to have enough auditors trained so that the auditors will not audit their own area, and so that you are not pulling one person away from their work too often. A general guidance number is 10% of the total number of employees; an Organisation with 50 employees would train 5 auditors, an Organisation of 100 would train 10. However, for larger Organizations the ratio of Auditors would go down.

Look for employees that have strength in investigating issues and are good communicators. The better people skills the auditors have, the smoother and more effective your audits will be performed.

Different Types of Evaluation of Compliance

When evaluation of compliance is carried out as standalone function, related legal knowledge is crucial.

AUDIT TIPS

Audits are a Management System's best friend. Audit findings lead to improvement in the effectiveness and efficiency of the system. How can you make your audit program work for your organization?

Here are some tips to help get the most from your internal audits.

BEFORE AN AUDIT:

- Make sure the authority of the audit team is established. This will increase the cooperation from auditees

- Decide what areas of the Organisation will be audited and the frequency of the audits. Prepare a yearly audit schedule based on status and importance and communicate it to the relevant people

- Develop an audit plan.

- Decide what other audit resources are needed - checklists, other auditors?

Different Types of Evaluation of Compliance

- Determine the purpose of the audit

  o Is it an overview of the area being audited or is it to concentrate on a specific system within the area?

  o Is it to comply with government regulations, standards, internal procedures and system?

- Read the documents you will be auditing against. Know what they say. Develop questions to ask the auditees.

- Hold a meeting with the auditors to discuss the plan, purpose, and scope of the audit.

- Conduct an opening meeting with the auditees.

DURING AN AUDIT:

- Be professional at all times

- Avoid being judgmental.

- Follow safety procedures, clean room procedures, etc. and all other related procedures

- Explain the purpose of the audit to the auditees

Different Types of Evaluation of Compliance

- Answer questions or discuss compliance problems brought to your attention by auditees

- Be flexible - if you find a potential problem not within the scope of the audit - evaluate the potential risks of the problem if left unaddressed.

- Encourage honesty with the auditees.

AFTER THE AUDIT: (IMPLEMENTING)

- Hold an auditors meeting to discuss the closing meeting content

- Hold a closing meeting with all auditees involved with the audit

- First, point what was done well. Second, communicate the non conformances and ensure the auditees understand the non-compliance and what part of the requirements has not been met

- Establish and facilitate immediate closure of the finding

- Issue the audit report in a timely manner but the findings immediately. Don't forget it's likely to be a Legal breach

Different Types of Evaluation of Compliance

- Encourage auditees to decide on the corrective and preventive actions. Allowing auditees to have input will give them ownership in implementing changes

- Assist those responsible for completing the corrective and preventive actions and setting reasonable deadlines. The correct action deadlines may vary depending on the severity of the non-compliance

- Be available and willing to help the auditees

- Ask for feedback on how you and your audit team were perceived - adjust your approach if necessary

One last tip: Involve people!

Use audits as opportunities to train others. Ask for a volunteer (who is not an auditor) to walk through the audit process with you as an assistant. This will provide others with a better understanding of what audits are and why they are necessary.
Involving people creates a feeling that everyone is a vital contributor to the goal of the Organisation - compliance.

With the new documentation requirements (ISO9001) giving the responsibility of determining what documents are needed for control of processes, it will become part of the auditor's responsibility to determine if the necessary procedures and work instructions have been documented, i.e. a process map. How can an auditor determine if a process is controlled if there is no procedure or work instruction?

As an auditor, you must evaluate if the process is being performed consistently, with consistent and acceptable results. An auditor can do this by asking several people performing the process relevant questions. Ask the people the questions individually, so they do not influence one another's answers. If the process is in control, the answers will be consistent. Some sample questions:

- Can you explain the steps to this process?

- What evidence is there of legal and other requirements compliance?

- What measuring and monitoring is required for this process?

- What are acceptable ranges for compliance of the equipment?

- What are the acceptance criteria for the product?

Different Types of Evaluation of Compliance

- What records do you need to complete for this process?

- Ask enough people to give you a good idea of how much the process varies between each individual performing the process. If the answers vary, there should be a procedure. The need for a procedure will generally depend on the complexity of the process and the training of the people responsible for the process.

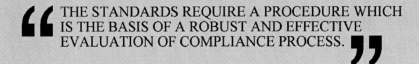

TOP TIP......

" THE STANDARDS REQUIRE A PROCEDURE WHICH IS THE BASIS OF A ROBUST AND EFFECTIVE EVALUATION OF COMPLIANCE PROCESS. "

Different Types of Evaluation of Compliance

CHAPTER 7

THE BEST WAY TO ACHIEVE

EVALUATION OF COMPLIANCE

So, there are many ways to satisfy evaluation of compliance, however, experience shows there are simple ways of achieving compliance with the full intent of meeting the clause requirements.

In my opinion, having audited the requirements of evaluation of compliance since 2004, there are easy ways and difficult ways to succeed.

One simple tried and tested approach follows.

This is the easy way…………

Always consider the distinction between evaluation of compliance and internal audit as completely different. However, some elements of evaluation of compliance can be covered by monitoring and measurement and internal audit usually through statutory inspection, the most important message is the need to maintain clarity between various functions so that at a point in time the status of evaluation of compliance can be demonstrated.

STAGE 1

From Chapter 3 - Firstly go to the Organisations applicable register of legislation and other requirements. Carry out a review of all listed requirements and ensure that it is comprehensive. When you are happy with the content, review each entry and apply a risk ranking to the entry based on that entry's significance to the Organisation. This is not a determination of applicability but an opportunity to establish how important the entry is to the Organisation.

You may wish to consider HIGH, MEDIUM, LOW (keep it simple). The procedure for evaluation of compliance of course will need to reflect what you decide is best.

Assuming you use HIGH, MEDIUM, LOW then determine a frequency in line with that, for example HIGH means the legislation is to be challenged, say four times per year, MEDIUM twice per year, LOW once per year.

This provides a level of objective evidence of having considered the significance of applicability of the applicable legislation and other requirements to the Organisation.

STAGE 2

The next stage is to create a schedule of all applicable legislation and other requirements – say down the left hand side of a page – and months of the already established management system/s cycle – across the top. This assumes that the principle of PLAN DO CHECK ACT is understood and being adopted. (See figure 4)

Many elements of a management system require a cycle to be established including, objectives and targets, internal audit, and of course evaluation of compliance. This allows effective cycle completion, output and review.

Typically management system cycles are 12 months – more than that tends to be a bit sloppy and less than too difficult to manage.

So you should have a manageable table or schedule of legislation and other requirements against months of the year and/or the management system/s cycle.

The Best Way to Achieve of Evaluation of Compliance

LEGISLATION	SIG	JAN	FEB	MAR	APR	MAY	JUN	JUL	AUG	SEP	OCT	NOV	DEC
H&S At Work Act	H	✓			✓			✓			✓		
Working At Height Regulations	H	✓			✓			✓			✓		
H&S (First Aid) Regulations	H	✓			✓			✓			✓		
Waste Regulations 2011	M		✓						✓				
Health & Safety (Safety Signs and Signals) Regulations SI1996/341	M		✓						✓				
Noise and Statutory Nuisance Act 1993	L						✓						
Climate Change Levy (General) Regulations 2001	L						✓						
Etc													

Figure 4 Evaluation of Compliance Plan

STAGE 3

Create another plan of legislation and other requirements by location i.e. where you are likely to find evidence of legislation and other requirements compliance. (See figure 5)

This could, for example be waste records, statutory inspection evidence, etc.

The Best Way to Achieve of Evaluation of Compliance

LEGISLATION	Stores	Goods Inwards	Site	Waste Management	Etc
H&S At Work Act	↘	↘	↘	↘	↘
Working At Height Regulations	↘	↘			
H&S (First Aid) Regulations	↘	↘	↘	↘	↘
Waste Regulations 2011			↘	↘	
Health & Safety (Safety Signs and Signals) Regulations SI1996/341	↘	↘	↘	↘	↘
Noise and Statutory Nuisance Act 1993		↘	↘		
Climate Change Levy (General) Regulations 2001	↘	↘	↘	↘	↘
etc					

Figure 5 Evidence by Location

STAGE 4

That's about it, now you have almost all of the tools needed to carry out a more effective evaluation of compliance.

It's just a case of getting on with it!

Of course that's the difficult bit, however with good planning and a systematic approach (which you now have), the task should be significantly easier.

The following model – which we call the "TEOC Approach™" (*The Evaluation of Compliance Approach),* describes typically the relationship between management systems and Evaluation of Compliance.

The Best Way to Achieve of Evaluation of Compliance

ENSURE EACH ENTRY IN THE REGISTER OF LEGAL AND OTHER REQUIREMENTS IS RANKED BASED ON SIGNIFICANCE

↓

BASED ON THE RANKING THE FREQUENCY OF THE CHECK CAN BE ESTABLISHED

↓

IDEALLY TREAT EVALUATION OF COMPLIANCE AS AN ACTIVITY ON ITS OWN

↓

IDENTIFY WHAT EVIDENCE OF LEGAL AND OTHER REQUIREMENTS NEEDS TO BE CHECKED AND WHERE

↓

CARRY OUT EVALUATION OF COMPLIANCE USING SUITABLY COMPETENT PERSONNEL & MAINTAIN RECORDS

↓

RESPOND TO ANY FINDINGS PROMPTLY AND PROVIDE ANALYSIS TO MANAGEMENT REVIEW

The Best Way to Achieve of Evaluation of Compliance

Figure 6 "TEOC Approach™"

FURTHER THOUGHTS

Of course, one of the most often asked questions is - "So what do I ask on a scheduled Evaluation of Compliance check".

Well that's as good as the overviews produced in the process of legislation and other requirements management. The overviews are key to the effectiveness of this as an overall exercise. If the understanding of what the applicable legislation is low, or nonexistent, then when you come to carry out evaluation of compliance it will be poor, if not nonexistent.

So, get the legislation and other requirements overviews established, understood and embedded in the system i.e. aspect evaluation and risk assessment, and subsequently operational controls and evaluation of compliance will become easy.

Another problem discussed further in Chapter 8, is the raising of non compliance during the evaluation of compliance process.

It is crucial that the same process for raising findings in the management system for say monitoring and measurement, and internal audit is not used. It is important that more pro activity is applied - you don't want to find a legal breach is documented for a period of time to resolve, and have a visit from a regulator in the mean time when it could have been dealt with.

EVALUATION OF COMPLAINCE REPORT					
Location of Evidence		Evidence Report Reference			
Date of Evidence Event		Carried Out By			
Legislation or Other Requirement					
Ref	Evidence Questions		Compliant	Non-compliant	Findings Ref
Accepted By		Date		Signature	
Non-Compliance Closed By		Date		Signature	
Evidence Notes					

Figure 7 Sample Evaluation of Compliance Report

The Best Way to Achieve of Evaluation of Compliance

TOP TIP......

- BREAK THE TASK IN TO SIMPLE STEPS LINKED TO PDCA

- ENSURE THE REGISTER OF APPLICABLE LEGISLATION IS COMPREHENSIVE

- RISK ASSESS APPLICABILITY - SAY HIGH, MEDIUM AND LOW

- CREATE PLANS FOR FREQUENCY, WHAT TO LOOK FOR

- TIGHTEN UP THE RESPONSE TO FINDINGS

The Best Way to Achieve of Evaluation of Compliance

CHAPTER 8

RAISING EVALUATION OF COMPLIANCE FINDINGS

It is very important to point out that NCRs, or findings raised as a result of the process of evaluation of compliance, need to be handled in a different way to findings raised by internal audit.

NCRs raised as a result of evaluation of compliance are an actual or potential breach of applicable legislation. Consequently they need to be closed as quickly as possible with absolute intent and related objective evidence. This is key to support clear evidence of identification and positive closure.

Management Systems Nonconformities typically arise due to one of the following:

1. The management system does not meet the relevant requirements of the particular standard requirement.

2. A supplementary requirement is not addressed, e.g. ISO 9001. ISO 14001, OHSAS 18001.

3. The Organisation is not in compliance with its own documented management system.

4. The system, either as a whole or in part, is judged to be ineffective.

However for the purpose of evaluation of compliance, it's easier than that. If there is a failure to demonstrate compliance with any part of applicable legislation or other requirement, then there is a non-conformity.

It is crucial that any finding identified as a part of an evaluation of compliance exercise, is closed as soon as possible – that could be as quick as immediate or by close of business to bring the Organisation back into compliance.

Lack of objectivity and preconceived ideas are the biggest constraints to effective auditing.

Raising Evaluation of Compliance Findings

Typical examples are nonconformities, raised due to lack of cross-referencing between documents and lack of work instructions to control the processes. In each case, these can result in the Organisation being forced to change numerous documents, sometimes at great expense, simply to satisfy the whim of an Assessor, who has not fully thought through the situation or looked at the specific requirements.

Some key points to consider when raising an Evaluation of Compliance Finding are:

1. Was the nonconformity evidence objective, and did the Auditor/Assessor <u>clearly</u> identify the <u>detail</u> to the auditee / guide?

2. Was the nonconformity justified – was it based on a clear legal or other requirements fact?

3. If the nonconformity was not raised, why was this?

4. Was the benefit of the doubt given where full objective evidence could not be uncovered?

Raising Evaluation of Compliance Findings

The raising of findings is a measure of the effectiveness of the management system and in the case of evaluation of compliance, a measure of compliance.

The first comment which could be made is; what do we mean by the "effectiveness of a management system". For the purposes of 3rd party certification this can be taken as "the degree to which the system meets the needs of management and more importantly, the needs of the recipient of the output of that system, i.e. end user".

The key here is the self regulation/improvement "tools" within the management system. These are the non-compliance control system, the corrective & preventive action system, the internal audit system and management review.

Non-conformities can appear from a variety of sources, e.g. customer complaints, 3rd party audits, 2nd party audits, and most importantly, internal audits / evaluation of compliance. Companies on occasions, intentionally or unintentionally "hide" customer complaints, therefore the Assessor should endeavour to look in the right places, should there be concerns.

However as previously expressed the source of non-compliance in relation to evaluation of compliance is easier. If there is objective evidence of non-compliance with a legal or other requirement, then there is a non-compliance.

No matter what the source of the non-compliance, it should be channelled <u>formally</u> into the corrective and preventive action system.

This system is, or should be, designed to find the reason or "root cause" of the non-compliance or breach. By addressing this cause properly, the chances of recurrence should be dramatically reduced.

Trend analysis should subsequently confirm this effectiveness (the ultimate aim of management).

REPORTING NON-CONFORMITY

The written non-conformity must be factual, and able to be substantiated by objective evidence. They should be referenced to the particular requirement, which could be:

- The related Legislation or Other requirement
- The management standard clause reference

- The Organisation's own system requirement reference.
- Supplementary requirement reference

All four references would apply in all cases.

There are instances where non-conformities are raised in which they can seem almost incoherent. References are often raised against the wrong piece of legislation, clause of the relevant management standard. The amount of text used may vary with the individual non-conformity, but should not be excessive. It should be concise but clear, using where possible the words of the legislation and/or requirement.

EVALUATION OF COMPLAINCE FINDINGS REPORT							
Location of Non-Compliance			Non-Compliance Reference				
Date Non-Compliance Issued			Raised by				
Proposed Closure			Role of Raiser				
Legislation Requirement Non-Compliance Raised Against							
Non-Compliance							
Accepted by		Date		Time		Signature	
Agreed Corrective Action							
Agreed Preventive Action							
Was action taken effective?				Yes		No	
CA / PA Date Closed		Auditors Name			Signature		

Figure 8 Sample Evaluation of Compliance Findings Report

71

Raising Evaluation of Compliance Findings

CHAPTER 9
FINDINGS FOLLOW-UP

The value of the audit and any findings must be assessed to assure that the findings and recommendations reflect compliance, workable and timely solutions, and have been achieved to some quantifiable degree to provide value to the organization.

Unfortunately, this does not happen as often as it should in practice.

THE BOTTOM LINE IS, HOW DOES AUDIT ADD VALUE?

Follow-up is the answer. If an organization is to understand what value audit can have to improving operational compliance integrity, efficiency and effectiveness. They must follow-up by looking at the prior evaluation recommendations of earlier work, auditors are able to assess if the Organisation has taken sufficient action toward the report recommendations.

If it has, a process is in place to assess what impact those recommendations had, and to formally report the assessment and findings. Often, auditors will receive direct feedback from managers,

Measuring Evaluation of Compliance

supervisors or staff that their actions were the results of an earlier findings report.

Based on the fact that a finding is a legal breach, then follow-up is critically important. Not only to demonstrate the finding has been closed, and the Organisation is now back into legal compliance, but also to provide evidence of effectiveness of the corrective and preventive action.

It is suggested that follow up is formal, and of course carried out as quickly after the finding has been raised.

The longer the time scale between the finding being raised and effective closure is critical, especially if it found that the closure is not effective.

Provide evidence of follow up in addition to the initial closure and maintain records for regular review, and to supply to the management review.

TOP TIP......

"" NON CONFORMITIES CANNOT FOLLOW THE
USUAL NCR REPORTING PROCESS IN LINE WITH
INTERNAL AUDIT - THERE NEEDS TO BE CLEAR
EVIDENCE OF IMMEDIATE CORRECTIVE AND
PREVENTIVE ACTION. ""

Measuring Evaluation of Compliance

CHAPTER 10

MEASURING EVALUATION OF COMPLIANCE

The measurement of evaluation of compliance can be a rather delicate subject – effectively you are declaring the level of non legal compliance of the Organisation!

However, there are many benefits of being able to demonstrate the status of evaluation of compliance at any point in time. It clearly demonstrates good control, not only to the Organisation, but to third parties.

Having considered a number of methods for determining the status of evaluation of compliance, from my experience, (as for the core process), keep it simple.

You may however, prefer to avoid trying to establish numerical measures as they can become an Objective and Target, which tends to have a negative impact.

Of course, being able to show how compliant or none compliant the Organisation is, will likely to be contentious. A numerical approach is certainly no exception, so it needs to be your choice. From my experience, it can present problems and draw criticism to the approach of Evaluation of Compliance.

Find a way of simply measuring the current status of evaluation of compliance, which best suits you and your Organisation. Maybe a measure of the number of findings based on numerical data, but shows GREEN, AMBER & RED bands. Anywhere in the GREEN band is considered acceptable and compliant, on the simple premise that any findings are brought immediately into compliance when found and raised.

CHAPTER 11

THE FUTURE FOR EVALUATION OF COMPLIANCE

Hopefully, the future is bright for Evaluation of Compliance! However, in the world of management systems evolution, if a clause is not clear, or well understood, it usually gets removed or demoted.

A fine example of this was management programme/s in ISO14001. This was a clause on its own when initially introduced, and due to the lack of understanding, it was tucked into the back of Objectives and Targets.

Legal and other requirements compliance is an integral part of Health and Safety, and Environmental top level commitment, and would be difficult to remove without significant dilution of the core principles of standards.

So with good intent at heart, I believe it will stay, and although it may have a change in clause wording, it will in essence deliver the same end result...

The Future For Evaluation of Compliance

ANSWER

From Page 14…………………

INPUT ➔ Where does it come from?

- It's an expectation from the standards
- Compliance with legislation is a common expectation

PROCESS ➔ What does it do?

- Defines the approach i.e. a procedure for carrying out Evaluation of Compliance

OUTPUT ➔ Whcrc does it go to?

- Management Review, as it expects evaluations to be evidenced at Management Review

Evaluation of Compliance Explained

Look out for the following titles by the same author

- *So I Ate the Table*

- *Tales of an Auditor*

- *More than a Badge on the wall*

Evaluation of Compliance Explained

BALKWELL LTD
ENGLAND
RAISING STANDARDS SINCE 1984

◆

MANAGEMENT SYSTEMS CONSULTANCY, AUDIT & TRAINING

David Balkwell can be contacted at

www.balkwellltd.com

Printed by
Book Printing UK
Remus House
Coltsfoot Drive
Peterborough
PE2 9BF